The Regifting of the Magi

[after O Henry]

Copyright © 2023 Alan Newton

All rights reserved. No part of this publication may be reproduced, distributed, or transmitted in any form or by any means without the prior written permission of the author.

Dedication

To my wife, Beverley

Acknowledgment

Thank you to William Sidney Porter, for your inspiration

Joe peered through the curtains onto the humble street of the former council estate that he regarded as home. It was hardly a Christmas card vista: everywhere overcast, dank and dreary, the grey and naked terrace opposite, a mirror-image of his own modest abode, seemed to cower in the cold; the pebble-dash cladding serving as the goosepimples of the underdressed and cold dwellings. Little festive cheer was in view, save for the gaudy lights of the end house, Number 51, but Joe suspected they were cover for the cannabis factory that was hidden in its loft space and disguised its abnormal electricity consumption. Certainly, the furtive flow of human traffic along its ginnel were not likely to find themselves on Santa's 'Nice' list, he concluded, but he was careful not to poke his nose into these surreptitious shadows of the estate, he and Marnie preferring to keep themselves to themselves, for in each other their world was complete and sufficient.

Not that Joe hadn't occasionally been tempted to explore the black economy of the estate. His income as a delivery driver was sorely limited, even at this time of year. After paying the rent and their other outgoings, including the MOT on his old van, his disposable income was, well, disposed of, pretty much. He fumbled in his jeans to examine his cash-flow status. Four one-pound coins, some silver shrapnel and a tangle of elastic bands from yesterday's deliveries was all he could excavate. Marnie had emptied the last of her own savings to buy the modest comestibles that currently sat in their second-hand fridge – at least they would enjoy a Christmas dinner tomorrow, their first since moving out of Marnie's mum's house into their own flat, and their first Christmas alone together. He should be elated, but instead he despaired that he had no present for Marnie, nothing that would befit and be deserving of the love of his life as they celebrated their first independent Christmas.

Marnie's mum had always thought him a 'waste of space' and in his darker, more insecure moments he feared she was right, although Marnie herself never doubted him or showed him anything but unconditional love. It certainly wasn't an equal partnership financially, and Marnie had more talent in her cute little piggy than he had in his entire being. She was out training now, pounding out the miles even into the darkening afternoon of a dreich Christmas Eve. If she were to shave even half a minute off her PB in the next few months, she could be in contention for the UK athletics team next year – an Olympics year – which would bring much-needed sponsorship and security. She would be able to give up her job at the supermarket and train full time, enjoy a proper athlete's diet and get some decent kit, including those ridiculously expensive high-spec running shoes she hankered after.

She might even buy a proper chain for the medal that she always kept around her neck for luck when training: an actual Olympic bronze medal, awarded to her beloved grandfather for the 50-Kilometre Walk at the '64 Tokyo Olympics. Though now long forgotten in the annals of British sporting history, at the time his third place in the heat and humidity of Japan had been not so much a surprise as a miracle. Grandpa Don was a wonderful example of a dying breed: a working-class amateur sportsman who had achieved on a world stage, despite holding down a regular manual job and training between shifts at the flour mill. A thin streak of a man, with lean, wiry muscles even into his eighties, matching his NHS metal-rimmed round spectacles, but with a heart as big as Santa Claus's belly and an inspirational beacon to Marnie which shone constantly over her own sporting odyssey.

Joe flopped onto their sofa to wallow in his gloom, being careful to avoid the saggy bit in the middle, but as always, this outmoded cast-off lifted his mood. A prize catch from the charity shop in the town centre – he and Marnie had carried it all the way from the high street (his van was, as usual, off the road at the time) and they drew many alternately amused or disdainful looks as they heaved it for two whole miles to their sparsely furnished flat. He had been deeply embarrassed, but Marnie had giggled the whole way, pausing only for fits of hilarity. How he loved her smile and infectious laughter. The memory made him both cringe and smile.

However, Joe's smile rapidly faded as the winter light dwindled and his impoverished predicament once again imposed itself on his mind and heart. He resorted to his fall-back consolation and solace. Ultimately, he was a resilient soul. He couldn't run for miles like Marnie, and he did not possess her confidence and gregarious nature, but he was invariably optimistic and never stayed down for long. Now, he rose for his bundle of keys which were on their dining table, another salvage treasure, and went to unlock a dilapidated old blue case in the corner of the room. It was hardly a secure locker, being composed of little more than plastic covered board, but the unlocking of it was a fitting ceremony commensurate with the treasure it contained.

Lifting up the lid of the storage case, Joe very carefully picked out his most valuable possession, holding it gingerly by the edges. A white Christmas was as unlikely as ever in this part of the country – no sentimental Dickensian tableau on this estate – but Joe never failed to be awed by the brilliant whiteness of the fragile treasure now framed by his hands which tenderly cradled the still pristine edges of a rare masterpiece. Joe rested the album in the crook of his left arm while he tenderly caressed the angled and embossed Helvetica lettering in the corner of the sleeve: "The Beatles."

Joe sighed contentedly as he reached into his back pocket for his old i-phone and sank again into the dubious comfort of the old couch. He called up a recording of 'While My Guitar Gently Weeps' on YouTube (he couldn't afford a music streaming service) and his eyes glistened in the gloom of the room as he listened to George Harrison's composition on his phone while he undressed the precious vinyl record with all the care of a Sotheby's auctioneer, lacking only the white gloves. He held the platter with his spanned hand like a silver-service maître d', while he imagined a diamond-tipped stylus kissing the grooves to produce the beautiful clarity of Harrison and Clapton's Gibson Les Paul guitars. Of course, Joe owned no turntable or proper sound system on which to play his cherished heirloom, so imagination substituted for the authentic hi-fidelity experience.

The album was the only thing left from his own beloved and long dead maternal grandfather, Granddad Graham. Presented to him on his fifteenth birthday after, he later discovered, his grandfather had been diagnosed with Stage 4 lung cancer, the old boy had said: "Look after it, our Joe – one day it'll be worth a bob or two. It's an original, you know; it belonged to m'dad!" And so it was: complete with a low 'limited edition' printed number (0000027), the original Apple label logo and the original photographic inserts of the 'Fab Four'. Steve, at *Vinyl Heaven*, had offered him a hundred and fifty quid for a it a year ago, but Joe knew it was worth a lot more than that. There wasn't a scratch on it and it hadn't been played for at least twenty years.

Harrison's high tones rang out from Joe's 'tinny' old mobile, and again he was jolted back to the present:

I look at you all, see the love there that's sleeping
While my guitar gently weeps
I look at the floor and I see it needs sweeping
Still my guitar gently weeps

It was at that moment that Joe had his epiphany. He had to catch his breath as his heart suddenly quickened and his arms trembled slightly as the realisation suddenly dawned upon him as to what he could do, what he *would* do, to make this the best Christmas ever for Marnie. He hurriedly but carefully re-dressed the precious disc into its sleeves and cover and then did the same for himself. The latter was easier for he owned few winter layers. Locating a 'bag for life' from under the kitchen sink, he eased his treasured cargo into its safekeeping.

Within minutes he was out the door and speed-walking like Grandpa Don towards the town centre shopping precinct, being careful to hold the carrier bag steady so that it did not catch the icy December breeze and flap against his legs.

Steve was just beginning to prepare to shut up shop early at *Vinyl Heaven*, having decided that the last-minute Christmas Eve shoppers were unlikely to be music connoisseurs and would instead resort to the petrol station's limp flowers or over-priced booze for their thoughtless, belated purchases, rather than his emporium of tasteful nostalgia. He was surprised to see Joe hurrying towards him and not altogether pleased – Joe spent a lot of time in the shop browsing his racks, but he could never afford to buy anything, and also Steve had set his heart on a Christmas Eve drink at *The Dog and Crook* after he'd locked up.

"Are you still in the market to buy my White Album, Steve?"

"And a Merry Christmas to you too, Joe! What's this, I thought you said you could never part with your granddad's pride and joy?"

But Joe was in too much of a hurry to explain. The negotiations did not take long. Steve was flushed with Christmas spirit (that, or his lunchtime spliff in the back yard) and upped the valuation previously offered to £200. Joe had read somewhere online that low-numbered original White Albums had fetched five-figure sums, but right now he regarded that as merely Weimar Republic hyper-inflation; its true value was determined by his love for Marnie. He had just enough time remaining to get to the antiquated jewellery store at the bottom of the High Street.

Whether Mr Goldman, like Steve, had also partaken of some lunchtime stimulation, which was doubtful; whether his heart was filled with the light of Hanukkah, which was perhaps more plausible; whether he was intoxicated from making such a substantial transaction at the eleventh hour of the festive shopping season, which could not be discounted; or whether he was touched by the story of this young man, and still remembered the warmth of the flame of first love for his Ruth when he was as green as the youth before him, we cannot say, but he did sell to Joe a handsome solid chain of pure platinum, worth considerably more – *considerably more* – than the £204.70 that Joe was able to fumble excitedly onto his old glass counter. Suffice it to say that both men were infused with the joy of Christmas when the old-fashioned bell on Mr Goldman shop door rang for the final time that Christmas Eve as Joe stepped out to return swiftly to his unassuming flat, which needed no other Christmas decoration than Marnie's bright smile and her warm embrace.

He was back with enough time to throw together a simple dish of pasta, tomato sauce from a jar and cheese, ready for Marnie's return from her long run. She called it carbo-loading, or some such athlete's jargon. After a fifteen-mile stretch, she would be ravenous and would overlook Joe's limited culinary skills. They would have a romantic dinner, just the two of them. They could even crack open that Prosecco that Marnie had been given by her work's Secret Santa, and afterwards he would present her with his gift in its handsome presentation box that Mr Goldman had thrown into the deal.

As the pasta dish simmered gently on the hob, Joe switched on their one table-lamp and lit some tea-lights that Marnie kept for their 'quiet nights in'. Again, he peered out onto the street to look for her return. She was later than he expected. She must have taken it at a gentler pace today; no point in risking injury during winter training, he supposed. The outrageously fluorescent Santa at Number 51 oscillated on the wall of the dealers' den, giving the impression of

Santa waving directly at Joe. Suddenly, Joe felt a knot of doubt in his stomach: what if Marnie were cross with him? They had often fantasised about saving a deposit to buy a place of their own; if he were going to part with his one thing of value, he could have put the money towards that. And she would certainly be angry that he did not get a four-figure sum for it. After all, Ringo's own personal copy (0000001) had apparently fetched $790,000 at auction. If that were a yardstick ...

But his anxious cogitation was interrupted by a taxi pulling up outside: a rare sight in this neighbourhood. Even more surprising, out of it stepped Marnie. "Oh Lord," he thought, "I hope she didn't turn an ankle on her run. So why didn't she phone me?" But she was moving freely as the cab driver helped her to unload several boxes from his boot and carry them up the path to the front door that they shared with the old couple upstairs. Joe was perplexed but quickly came to and moved to greet her.

"What's going on?" enquired Joe anxiously, as Marnie reversed herself through the door of the shared entrance lobby with the largest of the boxes, closely followed by the cabbie with two other containers. "Are you hurt? Why didn't you call me? What are these boxes? How could you afford a taxi?"

"All in good time!" trilled Marnie, reassuringly, as she counted out the fare and a (too) generous tip to the taxi driver. "Why don't you put the kettle on, while I sort out my surprise for my Best Boy!"

Joe reluctantly retired to their tiny kitchen to boil the kettle, still confused and not a little disappointed that she had not seemed to notice the romantic ambience that he had tried to create in their only living room. He realised too that he had not even noticed what was printed on the boxes. If they were a Christmas present of some kind, she had certainly not had time to wrap them, but he was not very observant (as Marnie's mum had often opined). He fired questions through the kitchen door which she would not allow him to open despite his entreaties. The girlish excitement in her voice was his only reassurance as she tore open cardboard and pulled at screeching polystyrene while explaining that she had abandoned her run after six miles because she had had a wondrous brainstorm. Instead, she had spontaneously veered off to town and gone Christmas shopping, still in her running gear.

"But how could you go Christmas shopping when you never carry valuables, other than your mobile, when you're out training? And anyway, you'd spent the last of your money in ASDA yesterday, buying the turkey crown, and how could you possibly afford a taxi…?"

He was cut short by the kitchen door being flung open and Marnie animatedly jigging up and down right in front of him while commanding him to shut his eyes and "no peeking"! She led him by the hand over to their dining table by the window. She deftly moved behind him, slipped her arms under his and covered his eyes with her own soft hands, still cool from the outside chill. She pressed her face into his back and squeezed him tightly.

"Promise you won't be mad with me?" she implored. "I know it's an extravagance, but I couldn't bear the thought of our first Christmas together without getting you a special present, without you finally being able to enjoy your favourite band, as they should be heard, and in the comfort of your own hearth … well, sort of!"

She released him and swivelled round to face him to delight in his surprise, still hugging him close. He blinked a couple of times to adjust his eyes to the candlelit room and then he stared in disbelief at the assembled splendour on their dining table. His lips parted, but he could make no sound. He half turned his head to her to say something, anything, but he could not move his eyes away from the gorgeously sleek ebony and titanium apparition that seemed to stare back at him, almost disapprovingly, as if it resented finding itself in these unaccustomed and inferior surroundings. He recognised it instantly, of course – the clean, sharp lines, the geometric perfection, the elegant handsomeness of the heavy polyoxymethylene platter sitting regally on a perfectly flat, impossibly smooth titanium platform: a Cambridge Audio turntable. He had never actually been this close to one before; he'd only ever drooled over a review article in a well-thumbed copy of *What Hi-Fi?* magazine that he kept in his van's glove compartment, borrowed indefinitely from his dentist's waiting room. It was a thing of beauty. Again, he was transported to somewhere else as he ached to touch the sleek black toner arm, but then, the lambent pink reflection from Number 51's Krack Kringle flickered and blinked him back to the present; he suddenly realised that Marnie was no longer wrapped around him.

She had giggled at Joe's apparent rapture, just the effect that she had dreamed of, and now she was on her knees rooting in his precious vinyl storage case, flipping through the meagre contents, eagerly searching for his Holy Grail. Finally, he would get to play his precious Beatles' album on equipment that Paul McCartney himself would be proud to use.

"Joe, I can't find your White Album? Why is it not in this case? Have you put it somewhere else for safekeeping?"

She looked up to find him staring down at her, with an expression that she could not read, and she began to feel anxious. His previous entrancement may not have been an overjoyed reaction after all, and her feminine senses were tingling with concern. In his left hand, Joe was holding out a long, slender case of faux soft black leather.

Marnie slowly rose on her strong distance-runner's legs, perfectly in control of her physical balance as she struggled with the emotional turmoil that was churning within her. No words passed between them as she gently took from him the black case and felt its weight. Tears were already welling in her eyes as she opened the lid to reveal the simple but aesthetically beautiful contemporary design of the pure platinum chain. She understood everything in that instant; her fears were confirmed. Joe's eyes and face were also dewed with apology for his profligacy and yet with anticipation that she might yet forgive him when she introduced the chain to her grandpa's heirloom.

Marnie flung her arms around Joe's neck, buried her head in his chest and sobbed breathlessly for what seemed a long time although it was just a few seconds of heartbreaking agony. Joe in turn enfolded her in his arms and pressed his face into her fragrant hair, still scraped back into a pony-tail from her run. After a few moments, Marnie resurfaced and gulped for breath as if she had been submerged and drowning. She wiped snot and tears away with her arm and clutched her beloved firmly by his temples, looking intently into his eyes.

"Merry Christmas, Joe! Let's put our presents away for now and keep them for a while. They're too nice to use just at present. You see, I pawned Grandpa's medal to get the money to buy your sound system, but the guy liked me and said he wouldn't know where to sell it on without doing a lot of research, so he'll most likely just keep it in his safe for quite some time. I'm sure it'll still be there in the New Year ..."

She sniffed loudly, her bottom lip quivered, and she fell silent.

"Tell you what," she said, eventually, "why don't we eat the pasta – mmm, it smells good! – crack open the Prosecco and snuggle down to watch *It's A Wonderful Life* on my old laptop? And then, how about an early night?"

"Sounds great, babes," he said, gathering her up in his arms once again. He clenched his jaw to contain his emotion and gazed again out the window. At that moment, three hooded youths skulked past the flashing Santa and disappeared down the ginnel of Number 51.

As you know, the Magi were the three wise men who brought gifts to the infant in the stable. It seems they started the tradition of giving Christmas presents. Do most people even know what frankincense and myrrh are these days? Can you buy them on Amazon? No doubt the Magi made wise choices for their gifts, and they were clearly expensive. Were Joe and Marnie wise to part so freely with their most precious possessions? Perhaps not, but maybe they were the wisest of all. Grandpa Don and Granddad Graham knew they couldn't take those same gifts with them when they were about to shuffle off this mortal coil, so they gave them to the ones they loved. Maybe Joe and Marnie did not realise the true market value of their heirlooms, but their sacrifice for love and the value of what they gave to and received from each other on their first Christmas together could not be measured, neither in denarii nor dollars.

The Promise of Youth

The modest, unassuming 1950s bungalow sat in the lee of the slope of the cul-de-sac peeking out at the other, almost identical bungalows that lined the street of Lime Tree Grove. Number 48, however, was a somewhat shabbier version than its neighbours, for it was occupied, as it had been for over forty years now, by nonagenarian widower, Gordon, who had long since retired his DIY tools to his dilapidated old garden shed at the rear of the property, and it was even longer since he had concerned himself with *fashionable* home improvements. And thus, the once bright vermillion roof tiles were now more of a burnt umber hue, the white paint on the original metal window frames more of a clotted cream colour and the thick old layers of emerald green paint on the superfluous metal gate to the side path were blistered and flaking, exposing the rusting iron underneath.

The two features that contrasted with the dated building in their brightness and quirkiness were Gordon's rose bushes – which he still fiercely pruned himself every winter, cutting them back hard to their grey, woody branches – and his single privet hedge, which he had fashioned into some kind of Hepworthian abstract design over many years:

an evergreen vortex of tightly packed leaves which no doubt was intended to complement the iron gate, once upon a time. The modernist boldness of the hedge design was probably considered daringly modern for this suburb in the last century, but now the vista betrayed dated tastes and spoke volumes about the vintage of the occupant.

Andrew was momentarily distracted by the solitary magpie perched on Gordon's now redundant television aerial, in turn sat on the similarly out-of-work chimney, as he strolled across the road to pay his now routine daily visit to his old neighbour. The warning cry of the magpie seemed to be to no other creature in particular, and Andrew somewhat resented its apparent alarm given the amount of food that he and his wife put out daily for the wildfowl in their neighbourhood. Since taking retirement from the teaching profession, Andrew had sort of adopted Gordon as his personal charity project. Andrew had spent all of his professional life in public service and in helping others, so he found it hard to resort to the golf course or binge on box sets when he could still be of use to someone else.

Additionally, Gordon was a wily old bird: long since widowered, and considerably neglected by his adult daughter and her family, Gordon continued to live independently by buying in some services from his pension (cleaning, laundry, garden) but also carefully grooming his various neighbours for miscellaneous other services (food shopping, trips to the Post Office to pay bills, resolving analogue problems in an increasingly digital world, and so on). He was careful to stagger his calls for help and not take advantage of any one kind neighbour, so that he never became a nuisance or a subject of frustrated gossip within their little enclave.

Andrew let himself in via the kitchen door, as was their custom. Today, he was surprised to find Gordon had a visitor.

"This is Ronnie," said Gordon, pointing to the handsome, twenty-something year-old sat on the underused floral-patterned settee that occupied the middle of the living room. "He's my adult social worker."

Andrew assumed that Gordon's recent stay in hospital, owing to a chest infection, had led to the authorities insisting on him having some kind of home help upon his discharge. The young lad seemed endearingly old-fashioned to Andrew's eyes, anachronistically dressed as he was in a beige woollen tank top with a matching crocheted tie. His baggy Oxford trousers, complete with turn-ups, and brogue shoes complemented the vintage look that he was clearly cultivating. The severe *Peaky Blinders* haircut of his thick blonde mop certainly completed the quaint ensemble. Only a chipped front tooth marred his good looks, marginally, and that would have been less noticeable had the lad not a propensity to smile broadly nearly all the time.

The two men shook hands. Andrew was surprised at the cold, leathery feel to Ronnie's skin as their hands clasped in greeting. He surreptitiously glanced at the young man's hand as they resumed their seats. It looked as though he had burn scars on his right hand, which seemed to extend underneath his shirt cuff.

Gordon was nestled in his usual threadbare armchair, which was adorned in antimacassars and yesterday's newspaper. He was looking frail: his back hunched over, liver spots visible through his thin white hair, his saggy wattle of throat skin unshaven and his bony knees angularly poking at the worn corduroy of his old trousers. Spread out on the heavy, mahogany coffee table between the two men was a photo album and other mementoes from Gordon's war years. He had served in the RAF, in a ground crew for Lancaster bombers in World War 2, having been called up in 1942, as soon as he was of age to serve. Andrew had himself enthusiastically perused Gordon's memorabilia many times before, being a former History teacher and genuinely interested in the old boy's treasures, and always a little regretful that he had never properly interrogated his own mother about her war years in the ATS, while she was still alive.

As one might expect of a social worker, Ronnie was quite skilled in drawing the old man out and asking the right questions about his experiences:

"So, you fellows would be out on the runway when the flight crew got the call?'

"Oh yes," agreed Gordon, "Those 'fly boys' were always a bit full of themselves, but they knew that they depended on us to service their kite and turn it around each day without missing anything. It would have been tragic enough to be pranged by German tracers, but how much worse would it have been to go down because of engine failure. Can you imagine! We always accompanied them to the runway to wish them luck and remind them that *our* aircraft was only on loan and that they shouldn't break it!"

"Yes indeed," Ronnie encouraged, "And it was pretty cramped in that aircraft, wasn't it?

"Ooh yes," purred Gordon, warming to his theme. "D'you know, the Pilot had to use his parachute as a seat, there was so little room. The Bomb Aimer would be lying on the floor, in a prone position, and the Gunner would have to block him in and put his parachute outside, because there wasn't room for it!"

"And the Navigator would have to climb over the main spar of the aircraft to get to his position," added Ronnie.

Andrew complimented Ronnie on his knowledge, saying how refreshing it was that a boy of his generation should take a keen interest in such things. If only his own students had been as enthusiastic about history! Although Andrew had come over to read Gordon's electricity meter for him, he found himself absorbed in their conversation. He pulled out photographs on his phone of the interior of a Lancaster bomber that he had taken on a school trip to the Imperial War Museum in London the previous year.

Gordon had seen these photos before, but it was moving to see the heads of the old veteran and the young social worker almost touching as they shared the i-phone and peered at the inner tangle of cables, pipes, tubing, dials, cogs and levers, while Gordon explained to Ronnie the different roles within a bomber ground crew, from fitters to electrical mechanics, from instrument repairer to radio mechanic to bomb handler. Ronnie nodded sagely and seemed to be concentrating intensely on the old man's narrative. He reciprocated by pointing out to Gordon where the Wireless Operator sat and where the Navigator sat, just beyond him, facing the port side of the aircraft.

"I used to make a lot of model aircraft when I was a boy," Ronnie explained, almost sheepishly, when Andrew again raised a surprised eyebrow at the detail of his knowledge.

"Oh, it was lovely to hear those four Merlin engines cough into life," mused Gordon, as he returned his attention to a picture in the photograph album of himself together with his mates on some long defunct Lincolnshire airfield.

"But even better when they returned and the surviving flight crew was stood down for a night or two?" suggested Ronnie.

" 'Stood down'? I haven't heard that term used for many a year," said Gordon, wistfully, "but yes, they were good times. We used to have dances when there was any kind of respite, you know, and we'd turn one of the hangars into a dance hall. In those days, you made your own entertainment, so there were always enough chaps who could play an instrument and they would somehow put together a dance band. They did a good job of impersonating the professionals: Glenn Miller, Joe Loss, Bert Ambrose … There was always plenty of beer, and the girls …!"

"Yes, the girls!" echoed Ronnie. "There were the girls who worked in signals, and the girls who worked in catering, feeding the chaps …"

"Always terribly sad when you'd come down to breakfast and there would be empty tables and chairs of a crew who hadn't returned the previous night. The girls would be weeping as they served the porridge," added Gordon, who was now on an emotional rollercoaster.

Ronnie seemed lost in thought for a moment. Then he said, "Yes, poor Joan! I wonder what became of her?"

"Joan?" queried Gordon, coming out of his own nostalgic reverie.

"Oh sorry," said Ronnie, "I, er, thought you said your girl at the time was called Joan?"

"No," corrected Gordon, "I had my share of popsies," he chuckled. "There were some benefits to being in a war, you know – but I didn't get married until after the war, to my *Joyce*. You know, I served in Egypt towards the end of the war and was posted to various places before being demobbed, but I still ended up marrying my childhood sweetheart."

Gordon withdrew into himself once again. Ronnie seemed embarrassed at his faux pas. Andrew had been watching their chemistry with increasing fascination. All three men fell into a momentary silence.

Ronnie broke the stillness: "You've got to hand it to those pilots, though, haven't you! They were a whizz at flying those things. Did they ever show you how to do the evasive 'corkscrew' manoeuvre to shake off those Messerschmitt 110s?"

Gordon and Andrew each gave him a look inviting him to continue.

"You put full aileron on," explained Ronnie, miming the actions, "You'd put the stick right down to about 360 miles per hour, and when you got to the bottom, you'd pull the bloody thing like that –" Ronnie leaned back and mimed the action he was describing with appropriate theatrics. "Took some effort, mind you! And you'd pull it up the other side." He mimed what would happen to the aircraft – the 'corkscrew' – using his scarred hand to represent the plane.

Even Gordon was pulling a bemused face at this level of expertise.

"Ha!" laughed Ronnie, realising his audience's inquisitive stare. "You see, I play a lot of video games and flight simulators. I think I need to get out more!"

"I'm going to be travelling myself next summer," he resumed, changing the subject. "Funnily enough, I've always wanted to visit Germany. I've only ever flown over it. There's a group of us going to go back-packing around the country, starting at Nuremberg. I've already booked my flight. I'm going to fly from the Midlands, over Denmark and the Ruhr Valley, and on to Bavaria. Wouldn't it be wonderful if you could come with us, Gordon!"

Andrew laughed. "I think Gordon's travelling days are over, Ronnie. I keep offering to drive him to visit Joyce's grave, but it seems he's lost a bit of confidence. Isn't that right, Gordon? You used to come over to my house to watch the football; now, you won't even cross the road to do that. It's such a shame, and you know I'd escort you over and back and look after you."

Gordon was a little flushed and muttered some excuse about his 'water-works' and his knees not being what they were. "I must regretfully offer my apologies. Thank you, all the same." Ronnie saved him from his embarrassment by rising and announcing that he needed to be on his way. "Other clients to attend to!" he declared.

Just before leaving, Ronnie stooped down to tidy the coffee table. From the assorted documents, he picked up the latest Christmas edition of the RAF Veterans' Magazine that Gordon received biennially through the post and handed it to Gordon. "Don't mislay this, Gordon. It's the one that was delivered today, and did you see that there's an illustrated feature on your old base in Lincolnshire that should be of particular interest. You might even see yourself in there."

Andrew saw him to the back door. He was quietly impressed with the young man and how he had so quickly bonded with Gordon. Knowing how stretched social services were, Andrew suspected that the lad had stayed on longer than his due slot to chat further in his own time. As he watched Ronnie unlatch the old metal gate, Andrew noticed that the solitary magpie was still on the roof, this time brazenly sitting on the guttering just feet away from the receding figure. Surprising – normally they are so skittish, thought Andrew.

He returned to the living room to find Gordon reading the magazine intently, but his rapture was interrupted by firstly, a tickly cough, which soon developed into alarming convulsions. It was another hour before Andrew was reassured that Gordon was sufficiently recomposed and could be left alone. He had clearly exhausted himself in reliving his past with Ronnie. During that hour Andrew made Gordon a cup of tea, read his electricity meter and tidied away his souvenirs and photographs. He tucked the magazine into the photograph album.

The next day, Andrew was alarmed to see an ambulance parked outside Gordon's bungalow. As he was closing his own front door to go across and enquire after the old fellow, Gordon emerged through the front door of his home in a wheelchair, carried down the steps by two burly paramedics, who informed Andrew that they were taking him in "as a precaution."

"Would you mind telephoning Dorothy, Andrew, and letting her know where I am? I would be most grateful, as always," said Gordon, wheezy, but impeccably polite, as usual. Dorothy was the insouciant daughter. The resident magpie looked on from a nearby telegraph pole.

A week later, Andrew was crestfallen to learn from another neighbour (not Dorothy herself, of course) that Gordon was never coming home again. His chest infection had turned into pneumonia and his heart had not been strong enough to take on such a formidable foe. He breathed his last in an intensive care unit at the age of ninety-five.

Gordon's few surviving friends and neighbours were not invited to the perfunctory private family funeral. It was not long before Dorothy and her brood had put the bungalow up for sale, hired a skip and were house-clearing with unseemly haste, enthusiasm and profligacy. Had he been such a bad father to deserve to have his earthly possessions treated in this way, wondered Andrew? Ornaments, crockery, books, old vinyl records – all were tossed in the skip with careless abandon.

Andrew felt a terrible sadness. He wanted to connect to someone else who would have cared about Gordon's passing. He suddenly remembered young Ronnie; he was sure that Dorothy would not have bothered to inform Adult Social Services of her father's demise. Strangely, however, the Council Offices' switchboard operator had not heard of Ronnie, when he phoned them, nor the duty manager when Andrew had insisted on being put through to the relevant department. It did not help that Andrew could not recall knowing Ronnie's surname, of course, but he was frustrated that some jobsworth at the Town Hall was unwilling to enquire further to locate their junior colleague. Andrew could only hope that Ronnie would be due to visit again soon and would knock on his door for information when he found Gordon's house shuttered and empty.

That same evening, when Dorothy and her vandals had departed from their de-cluttering duties, something impelled Andrew to go and inspect the brimming skip on Gordon's potholed driveway. He was not sure what he was looking for, but as he peered into the jumbled detritus of Gordon's life, his eye was caught by the faux leather cover of Gordon's wartime photograph album. He used two of Gordon's discarded old walking sticks like oversized chopsticks to carefully retrieve the album from the depths of the skip. How could anyone throw away such treasure, let alone a family heirloom? The magpie flew down onto the side of the skip and tilted his head at Andrew, seemingly disapproving his 're-housing' of the photograph album. Andrew shooed the tiresome bird away. "None of your business, matey!"

Andrew later raised a glass containing two fingers of a fine single malt in salute to his late friend, as he settled down in his own living room to browse through the photograph album. He smiled at the black-and-white images of the Brylcreemed eighteen-year-old Gordon, and the pictures of the base football team that Gordon used to run in Egypt, all running around like mad-dog Englishmen, shirtless in the

North African sun. He was about to skip over a large, group photograph of the Lincolnshire base personnel, all positioned according to rank and role in and around a couple of Lancasters on the runway of the base, but he was curious to find Gordon in the throng, which he eventually did. At the same time, his eye was caught by a familiar-looking face within what was clearly a flight crew, sat together just a few yards away from Gordon's team. He quickly went to find a magnifying glass from his study to inspect the image more closely. It seemed like a bizarre doppelganger coincidence! Then again, those 1940s boys nearly all looked a bit alike in their monochrome uniforms with their slicked-down hair. He took a sip of his whisky and noticed some loose papers tucked inside the back cover of the photograph album, including the latest edition of the veterans' magazine about which Ronnie had been so solicitous, anxious that Gordon did not lose it. Andrew recalled him saying that the newsletter featured an article on Gordon's old base in Lincolnshire.

Andrew read with profound interest the feature article. Among the tragic recollections was a reference to the disastrous raid on Nuremberg in March 1944. Bomber Command were intending to flex their muscles and give Hitler a symbolic bloody nose by obliterating the birthplace of the Nazi party. Instead, it had been a disaster: the Germans had improved their defences and were ready and waiting. 96 planes were lost that night. The budding journalist/historian had done some thorough research, including lists of the casualties from Gordon's base in Lincolnshire and, taking up half a page of the magazine, a single, indicative photograph of one particular Lancaster crew which never returned from that Raid.

Whether it was the whisky that suddenly made Andrew's mouth dry and his back tingle, or something else, he would not be able to tell you, definitively. But as he studied the faces of the seven airmen of 452 Squadron Lancaster M-Mother *The Dortmund Devil*, his eyes fixed on the smiling, good-looking, blonde youth on the far right of the back row, with a distinctive mop of fair hair and a slight chip in one of his front teeth. It took an effort of will for Andrew to read the legend underneath:

"L – R, Back row: George Clarke (Bomb Aimer); Ernest Yeats (Wireless Operator); Charles Bennett (Mid-Upper Gunner); Ronald Turner (Navigator) ...

Printed in Great Britain
by Amazon